D0995635

persuasive reports and proposals

ANDREW LEIGH

Andrew Leigh is a partner in Maynard Leigh Associates, a leading training provider to many major corporations. An adviser to companies on team, leadership, and development strategies, he is also a Fellow of the IPD. He is the author of many management books, including *Effective Change* (1988) and *20 Ways to Manage Better* (2nd edn, 1995), both published by the IPD.

Management Shapers is a comprehensive series covering all the crucial management skill areas. Each book includes the key issues, helpful starting points and practical advice in a concise and lively style. Together, they form an accessible library reflecting current best practice – ideal for study or quick reference.

The Institute of Personnel and Development is the leading publisher of books and reports for personnel and training professionals, students, and all those concerned with the effective management and development of people at work. For full details of all our titles please contact the Publishing Department:

tel. 020-8263 3387
fax 0202-8263 3850
e-mail publish@ipd.co.uk

The catalogue of all IPD titles can be viewed on the IPD website:
www.ipd.co.uk

persuasive reports and proposals

ANDREW LEIGH

INSTITUTE OF PERSONNEL AND DEVELOPMENT

First published in the *Training Extras* series in 1997
Reprinted 1998
First published in the *Management Shapers* series in 1999

Design by Curve
Typesetting by Paperweight
Printed in Great Britain by
The Guernsey Press, Channel Islands

British Library Cataloguing in Publication Data
A catalogue record for this book is available from the
British Library

ISBN
0-85292-809-2

**INSTITUTE OF PERSONNEL
AND DEVELOPMENT**

IPD House, Camp Road, London SW19 4UX
Tel.: 020 8971 9000   Fax: 020 8263 3333
Registered office as above. Registered Charity No. 1038333.
A company limited by guarantee. Registered in England No. 2931892.

contents

Other titles in the series:

1 persuasive reports and proposals

There are three rules for writing a novel, Somerset Maugham claimed; the trouble is that no one knows what they are. The same applies to reports and proposals. There are plenty of principles, guidelines, and sources of advice. The problem is knowing what works and what does not.

Writing persuasively is an essential business skill. Most successful people in organisations communicate well in writing, and few people reach the top without learning the art. It is also immensely satisfying when what you have written has the desired impact.

What does being a persuasive writer mean? It is that people tend to do what you want because of what you have written; for example, they take action, agree, make decisions, call you.

Because you cannot be there in person, your writing must speak for you. There is no body language, facial expression, or other physical way of establishing your presence. Persuasive writers constantly experiment, learning as they go, discovering what works best for them.

Whether you are putting together a report or a proposal, the starting-point is always the same:

● Use plain English.

Persuasive business writing invariably consists of short, simple words and brief, easy-to-read paragraphs. No matter how complex the issue or how involved the material, you can always turn it into clear, readable English.

For help with producing plain English, consider attending one of the courses provided (for example) by the Plain English Campaign or read Martin Cutts' excellent *Plain English Guide* (see *further reading* on page 85). This *Management Shaper* goes rather deeper – into the murky realms of the art of persuasion.

Route map

Persuasive writers take you on a journey by telling a story, dramatising an issue, highlighting an opportunity. So let's begin! The route we travel during this *Management Shaper* involves five aspects of persuasive writing:

● purpose

■ reader

▲ image

◉ detail

● enhancers.

Each contributes to making your writing influential. Incidentally, the first letters of these five words combine into a simple reminder of how you should feel about your reports and proposals:

P-R-I-D-E

You will make your documents effective by taking the trouble to maximise their impact, using the ideas presented here. When you are finally ready to present your document, check whether you really feel a sense of pride in it. It is more likely to be persuasive when this is how you feel.

Why in writing?

No matter how powerfully written, a document can rarely achieve the same impact as delivering your message in person. Even reluctant verbal presenters are usually more persuasive than any document. Before fully committing yourself to a written presentation, be sure that you know why this is a better solution than an oral delivery. Always ask yourself: 'Why should the presentation be in written form?'

If you are fearful of doing it in person, invest in some formal presentation skills training. Conversely, it makes little sense to choose an oral presentation if all you are doing is reporting information. Often, though, it is wiser to call a meeting than prepare a time-consuming report. If your purpose is to persuade, consider a combination of submitting your document followed by an oral presentation.

The argument for a personal presentation is that your document cannot respond to questions or argue your case with energy. Documents are passive and can remain on a desk for weeks without being fully read. Adopt a written form of presentation only if:

- it is the most feasible means of reaching a scattered readership
- people will require time to absorb the contents
- an oral presentation is unacceptable
- it offers the best way of conveying your particular message
- it supports your verbal presentation.

Getting what you want

There are several basic ways of attempting to achieve what you want through writing:

- pure logic
- manipulation
- coercion
- persuasion.

It ain't what you say...

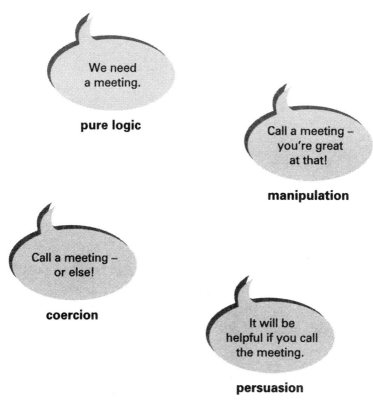

Many people believe that the way to persuade is solely through logic, convincing by sheer force of argument using factual communication. This approach assumes that 'The facts will speak for themselves.' Alternatively, you can attempt to get what you want by manipulation. This is when you imply false promises or threats. There may be no substance behind these, and so this approach may sometimes involve distorting the truth. Manipulation causes others to believe, perhaps wrongly, that there will be gains or losses from responding as you want them to do. A further alternative, plain coercion, is different, because here you make a real, unmistakable threat. 'Do as I say,' you warn, 'or there'll be trouble.' You may even explain the exact nature of the threat you are making:

- 'Give me a pay rise or I'll leave.'

- 'Failure to authorise the new system will have serious consequences.'

- 'Without this campaign we'll lose market share.'

A fourth approach, persuasion, encourages people to arrive at their own reasons for saying yes. That is, you find ways to allow them to reach their own decision, enabling them to feel more committed to actions, conclusions, and decisions.

Logic alone is seldom sufficient to win hearts and minds. Consequently, many technical experts who immerse themselves in detail often stumble when it comes to reports and proposals. Facts do not 'speak for themselves', because it matters which ones you select and how you present and interpret them – all this determines whether written material is persuasive.

On balance, persuasion is the most effective way of getting what you want, because people generally resist being manipulated and coerced. Occasionally you might succeed by being both manipulative and coercive, yet neither will enhance your reputation and, in the long run, these approaches tend to be unreliable.

The persuasion pyramid

To write persuasively it is essential to inject something of yourself into the material – see *The persuasion pyramid* below.

The persuasion pyramid

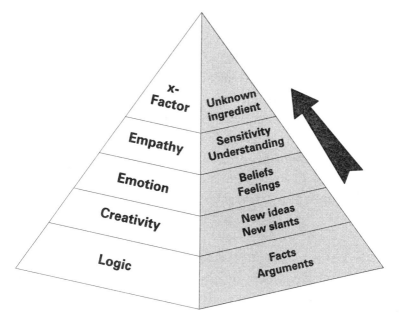

Most persuasive business writing rests initially on a foundation of logic, arguments, and facts that hang together and make intuitive sense to the reader. Yet this is seldom sufficient to make an entirely convincing case. You also need new ideas, a different slant – perhaps an alternative perspective. These require creative thinking and a willingness to make unusual connections.

Telling people what they already know is seldom persuasive. What ultimately persuades is when you add to their picture of the world.

Even the most technical reports or proposals deserve to contain your opinions, beliefs, feelings, or interpretations. Emotion plays a critical role. Although it is sometimes hard to strike the right note, the most persuasive documents convey a sentiment of some kind, such as excitement, pride, encouragement, anxiety, or commitment. Similarly, empathy is another powerful contributor towards making documents persuasive. Communicating sensitivity, awareness and understanding of a reader's situation encourages a greater readiness by the person to do what you want.

In any persuasive writing there remains an unknown factor that contributes to persuasiveness. It might be style, timing, the right readership, the way you present the material, a dash of coercion, or whatever. You cannot analyse and bottle this ingredient – which explains why persuasion is an art, not a science.

2 purpose

What do you want to achieve through your report or proposal? It might be to ask permission to do something, offer a deal, make a sale, open up a new opportunity, or suggest a solution. Reports that mainly present information are persuasive only if they also make suggestions and draw conclusions for action.

State your purpose as a single headline or statement

A useful discipline is to create a single headline or statement summing up your purpose. This encourages you to become clear about what you want to say. Try stating it as if talking to an intelligent 10-year-old, using simplified ideas and language.

Suppose you want a salary increase. You might initially conclude that your purpose in writing to your boss is to gain immediate agreement to the pay rise. But is it? Would you really expect this person, on receiving your suggestion, to authorise the resources immediately? Might not the real aim be to encourage a meeting to discuss your arguments for a pay rise? There is a genuine difference between these two statements:

● 'Pay me more money!'

■ 'Let's meet to discuss my case for more money.'

By focusing on the underlying reason for your document, you improve the power of its intention. When you first decide on the purpose of a report or proposal, it may prove to be too broad or imprecise to make an impact. For example, the following are statements of purpose that can be 'chunked' into more precise aims:

● I want a salary increase:

> Consider the case for a salary increase.

> Let's meet to discuss the grounds for a pay rise.

> Implement a pay rise at my next review date.

■ Act on this report:

> Consider the contents.

> Call a meeting to review the implications.

> Make a decision by...

▲ Introduce a new computer system:

> We need a new system; do you agree?

> Authorise a feasibility study.

> Agree to the first stage of a major investment.

Can you dissect the purpose of your next report or proposal in this way? See if you can tease out precisely what it is you are really asking of your reader(s). Also, in refining your purpose consider:

● Why am I telling them this now?

■ What effect do I want to achieve?

▲ What is the actual outcome I desire?

Answering the first question clarifies the timing of the presentation of your material. Occasionally you have no choice about when to present your document, yet often you remain free to decide this. Doing so on a whim is unlikely to achieve the persuasive effect you want.

The second question helps to clarify how you want your readers to feel: do you want them excited, worried, challenged, impatient, curious, annoyed, pleased? What effect do you want to obtain? Similarly, identify what effect you want the different sections of the document to create.

The third question helps to get clear in your mind what you would consider a successful outcome of a persuasively expressed report or proposal (see also Chapter 6).

The persuasion sequence

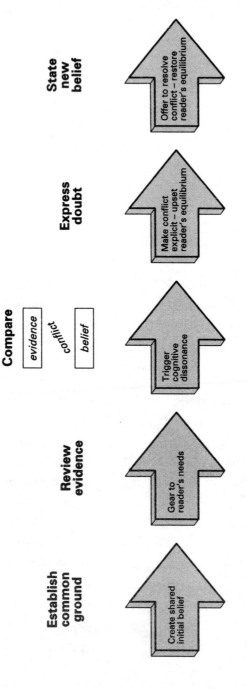

| Establish common ground | Review evidence | Compare | Express doubt | State new belief |

Compare

| evidence |
conflict
| belief |

- **Establish common ground** — Create shared initial belief
- **Review evidence** — Gear to reader's needs
- **Compare** — Trigger cognitive dissonance
- **Express doubt** — Make conflict explicit – upset reader's equilibrium
- **State new belief** — Offer to resolve conflict – restore reader's equilibrium

(Adapted from: 'Writing business correspondence using the persuasion sequence' by M Moran, *The ABCA Bulletin*, June 1984.)

The persuasion sequence

The persuasion sequence is a way of refining your purpose; it uses psychological research to guide the process of constructing an argument (see the illustration opposite).

The first step is to establish some common ground with your reader. Lack of this undermines the persuasive impact, so it is vital to get this starting-point right by learning as much as you can about the intended reader.

How do you establish common ground with your audience? One of the most powerful ways is by conveying a shared belief. For example, you might reveal that you both think the computer system needs reviewing, or that you both see a requirement for a new product, or that you should tackle an issue jointly.

The second step is to present the evidence. Tailor this to your reader's needs, not your own. You may feel that a vast array of facts will support your case, yet senior managers, for example, usually value seeing only the most important ones.

The third step in the persuasion sequence is to trigger *cognitive dissonance*. This is when the reader holds two conflicting positions that cannot be reconciled. For example, let's suppose that the other person believes that the computer system is fine, yet you present evidence to the contrary. Or your boss considers that you are well paid, yet you offer evidence suggesting otherwise.

Cognitive dissonance causes discomfort because it starts a mental battle between two or more irreconcilable situations. Consequently, the reader tries to eliminate or reduce the conflict so as to become more comfortable again. The only way to achieve this is by accepting that something must change. It is this that causes people to alter a strongly held view or become willing to consider a new alternative.

Having sown the seeds of cognitive dissonance, you prepare to reap the harvest. You express your doubts about the situation, giving your views. Unlike reliance on 'just the facts' to persuade, you draw attention to the difference between what the reader imagines the situation to be and how you see it. Again the reader is forced to face a situation that needs resolution. For example, you express doubts about the reliability of the computer system in the light of the evidence, or you suggest it might be time to reconsider your salary, given the new information about your present work.

In the final stage of the sequence, you offer a way forward – that is, you make decisions, offer suggestions, draw conclusions, submit recommendations. These offer to resolve the conflict created in the reader's mind, restoring the person's equilibrium. Once more the reader can feel comfortable because you have eliminated cognitive dissonance.

This persuasion sequence can help to guide your purpose and is worth adapting for your own use.

3 the reader

How do you climb inside someone's head? Making reports and proposals achieve what you want requires an effort to understand your readers. The more you know, the less you will be writing in a vacuum. Aim to identify the readership and therefore to:

● understand

■ anticipate

▲ respond.

Successfully putting yourself in the reader's shoes enables you to present your material from a position of knowledge and understanding instead of having to indulge in mere guesswork. The more accurately you do this, the greater will be your ability to persuade.

Identify

When you are first asked by someone to produce a report, you might assume that this person is your sole reader. You may in fact have others:

● Who will they be, and what do you know about them? Build a mental picture of each one.

What are their expectations and needs?

How much time are your readers likely to spare for absorbing your document? You cannot assume that it will be read from cover to cover. Some of the most persuasive reports and proposals therefore fit neatly onto one page. If longer than that, they are usually fronted with a one-page summary.

When are readers most likely to give the document their full attention? If possible, time its delivery to arrive at the most opportune and welcome moment. For example, if you know your boss always takes reports home to read carefully at the weekend, delivering yours on a Friday afternoon may prove good timing.

Understand

The most obvious way of discovering what it will take to persuade your readers is to ask. Try discovering from potential readers what might:

● convince them

■ concern them

▲ encourage them to agree

● make them say no.

If you cannot get access to a potential reader, find someone who can and invite the person to help you with your research.

Anticipate

Truly persuasive proposals anticipate:

● what resistance will occur

■ what questions will arise.

Determine what your reader is likely to find most and least important. Generally, it makes sense to present the most important items first and the least important ones later.

Because good anticipation arises through imagining yourself to be the reader, develop a clear mental picture of how this person looks and sounds. Try reading your draft document aloud slowly while 'listening' to what you imagine might be the other person's reaction.

● *Imagine one potential reader at a time.* You cannot 'listen' to everyone simultaneously, so imagine each person in turn, conducting a mental dialogue. Try to 'hear' in your mind what this person might say, how he or she would react, what questions he or she might ask.

■ *Visualise in detail.* Picture the reader's mannerisms, way of speaking, sitting, answering the telephone, fiddling with a pencil, brushing hair back and so on.

▲ *'Play' an imaginary scene in your mind.* Visualise the reader holding your report while speaking to the person's own boss on the telephone. How might the conversation go?

> Imagine the reader summarising the document and commenting on it: what would this person say?

Even if you hardly know your readers, an imaginary dialogue and the visualising process can prove helpful. For instance, when sending proposals to another organisation, try imagining the chairman giving a critical commentary to the selection committee. It all helps with improving your anticipation.

Bringing the reader alive in your mind is like an actor becoming immersed in a part. By partly 'becoming' the character of your reader, you begin appreciating how this person might react to different situations. It helps stimulate ideas about that person's:

● knowledge

■ opinions

▲ beliefs.

The more committed you are to an idea or a suggestion, the harder it becomes to stand back and conduct an honest mental dialogue with readers, to 'hear' their resistance, objections and so on. Consider asking someone who knows the potential reader well to role-play this person, putting forward what he or she believes would be said.

If your reader has strong opinions on something, these may influence the reaction to your document. What are these opinions? Even if you think they are wrong or misguided, by naming them and making them explicit you again improve your chances of writing more persuasively.

Gaining a feel for what might go on in another person's mind is mainly a matter of practice and experience. Try the test shown at the end of this chapter and, while doing it, see if you can also identify what principles of persuasion are at work. Compare your answers with those at the end of this *Management Shaper* (see pages 81–83).

Common ground

Chapter 2 introduced the importance of establishing common ground with your reader. You can do this by communicating such messages as:

- I like you.
- I respect you.
- I agree with you.
- I'd make that decision too.
- I understand you.
- I appreciate your situation.

- You were right.
- We have the same experience.
- We're both concerned.
- I trust your judgement.

These often need to be implicit rather than explicit, the reader learning how you feel from the way you present the material.

Sometimes it is worth making the message explicit so there is no mistaking your intention. For example, in a sales proposal you might demonstrate that you understand the customer's values, appreciate the latter's commitment to quality, and so on. You explain that you too hold these values, offering evidence to support this, explicitly mapping out common ground between you.

You can also establish common ground by doing something in the same way that your reader does. For instance, if the latter normally pays meticulous attention to detail and is extremely thorough, then reflecting these qualities in your document implicitly establishes common ground.

Similarly, if a reader commonly uses certain phrases, words, or concepts, then you might discreetly use them in your document too. This 'mirroring' of the other person is the equivalent of matching body language, which also builds rapport.

How readers read

What happens when people read? It may appear that they merely let the words flow over them, skipping pages or dipping randomly into them. Yet research shows that reading is not passive, because *the brain organises information to make sense of it*. This has important implications for understanding how readers think. Because people often do the organising subconsciously, you can actively help by:

- prioritising how information is presented

- achieving maximum clarity

- being selective about what to include and exclude

- explaining what should happen next.

Priorities

Research into reading habits suggests that it is best to structure documents hierarchically – that is, you present the reader with the most important information first and the less important information later. This enables the reader to proceed through the material from the top down, so be sure to provide headings, numbered sections, and bullet points.

- Put the subject first – that is, use active rather than passive sentences (see below).

- Include material that encourages readers to use their own ideas and knowledge – for example, offer choices, pose questions, suggest possibilities.

Don't leave readers guessing.

Clarity

Given that your document is in English, you are using one of the world's most flexible and adaptable languages. However, this also makes it possible for you to be misunderstood even if you are writing clearly.

'Clarity' simply means that the reader easily understands what you say and what you mean. The two are not necessarily identical. For example, when you suggest that something should happen 'immediately', to one person this could mean 'today' but to another 'within a week'. Looking for sources of misunderstanding is an important discipline in making any document fully persuasive and is part of the vital editing stage (see Chapter 6).

Clarity encourages readers to read through to the end, yet does not guarantee that your document will be persuasive. A lack of it, though, will certainly undermine its impact.

Selectivity

Selection of any material for a report or proposal is always a matter of judgement. Diligent but inexperienced writers tend to include absolutely everything that seems relevant and clutter up their documents with excess material.

Be selective on behalf of your reader by including only that material which significantly contributes to making your case or getting your message across. Keep hearing in your mind a critical reader asking:

● Do I really need to know that?

■ What am I supposed to do with this information?

Failed reports are usually full of 'nice-to-know' information doing little to advance the cause of persuasiveness.

The politeness factor

People in business seldom welcome inconsiderate, intemperate, or disrespectful behaviour; it usually adversely influences how they respond both in face-to-face encounters and written documents. Politeness in a document does not mean being obsequious or using flattery. It does imply having respect for your readers, using forms of language that they understand and showing that you care what they think. A

The politeness/clarity graph

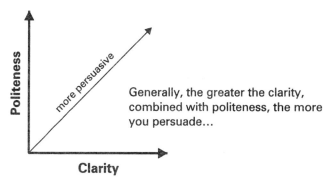

Generally, the greater the clarity, combined with politeness, the more you persuade...

mix of politeness and clarity makes intuitive sense and works well in practice (see the graph on page 23).

Demand attention

The average manager spends considerable time telephoning, being interrupted, attending meetings, and absorbing written material. Like you, your reader is bombarded daily with countless messages, images, and communications. If your material is to get the attention it deserves, take particular care over:

- the opener
- retention
- the closure.

The opener

The opener is literally your first sentence and paragraph. Give these your best creative effort, because people tend to make instant judgements based on limited information. A 'grabby' opener can set the tone for everything that comes later. Get it wrong and you start losing that crucial initial interest. Openers are fun to devise and are ideally:

- short
- easy to understand
- direct.

Retention

Having caught the reader's interest, do your best to keep it. Look for interesting ways to make the reader take notice such as:

- issuing a challenge

- summarising a problem

- stating the purpose

- using an interesting quotation

- presenting a powerful statistic

- telling a pertinent story.

The closure

Closure is also an important aspect of retaining the reader's attention and increasing awareness of your message. Many reports and proposals stumble here because the writer has lost energy and interest.

Successful closure ends your document memorably, engaging the reader's emotions and interest. Effective closures include:

- short summaries

- brief recommendations

- 'next-step' descriptions

- statements of commitment

● memorable phrases

● quotations

■ provocative questions

▲ pictures and images.

Conclusion

Getting 'inside' the reader is essential for influential writing. Researching readers so that you can do some of their thinking for them is a sound investment, allowing you to anticipate problems and objections that might otherwise block your proposals.

Exercise
How persuasive are you?

Read between the lines – what might be going on in the reader's mind?

1   You write one of these two sentences to someone:
    (a) 'You're doing a good job.'
    (b) 'Several people have been telling me you're doing a good job, and I agree.'

Which is more persuasive – (a) or (b) (*circle one only*)?

What thoughts might the reader have about both statements?

(a)

(b)

2 You write one of these two sentences to someone:

    (a) 'The project should proceed, but only if fully funded.'

    (b) 'The project should proceed when fully funded.'

Which is more persuasive – (a) or (b) (*circle one only*)?

What thoughts might the reader have about both statements?

(a)

(b)

3 Your boss writes to you: 'I expect you to have my report ready on time.' You reply with either of these two sentences:

    (a) 'I realise you're expecting my report on time, and I'll make sure it is.'

    (b) 'Naturally I'll deliver my report as agreed.'

Which is more persuasive – (a) or (b) (*circle one only*)?

What thoughts might the reader have about both statements?

(a)

(b)

4 Your boss writes to you: 'Do you think it's a winner? Shall we
   proceed?' You reply with either of these two sentences:
   (a) 'After much thought about whether we should proceed, I
       conclude that we should do so.'
   (b) 'Yes, I think it's a winner. Let's proceed.'

Which is more persuasive – (a) or (b) (*circle one only*)?

What thoughts might the reader have about both
statements?

(a)

(b)

5 You write to your boss either of these two sentences:
   (a) 'You've asked me to do this project and I'll try to bring it
       in on time.'
   (b) 'Thanks for letting me do this project; it'll be completed
       on time.'

Which is more persuasive – (a) or (b) (*circle one only*)?

What thoughts might the reader have about both
statements?

(a)

(b)

6 You write to a customer either of these two sentences:

    (a) 'If you give us this order we'll produce the results you want.'

    (b) 'Give us this order and we'll produce the results you want.'

Which is more persuasive – (a) or (b) (*circle one only*)?

What thoughts might the reader have about both statements?

(a)

(b)

7 Your boss writes to you: 'I can see no reason to invest in this new computer system.' You reply with either of these two sentences:

    (a) 'I agree that there would be no reason to invest in a new computer system so long as our present rate of growth slows down or ceases altogether.'

    (b) 'I completely disagree: we must have a modern system to cope with our present rate of growth.'

Which is more persuasive – (a) or (b) (*circle one only*)?

What thoughts might the reader have about both statements?

(a)

(b)

4 image

How things seem can prove even more important than how they really are. A document may have a sufficiently strong image to be highly influential despite being short on either facts or strong arguments. Image plays an important role in persuasion and includes:

- style
- tone
- spoilers
- appearance.

Style

A drug breakthrough described in the magazine *New Scientist* would be barely recognisable in the tabloid press. The difference extends beyond factual information into 'style', which is equivalent to using your personality in a verbal presentation. Creating your own style involves:

- seeking and responding to feedback
- experimenting with different ways of expressing messages
- learning from pitfalls.

Although style is partly a personal issue, it may also be a corporate one. Some organisations, for example, require written reports to have a particular format with rules on language, such as always using the third person – 'he' or 'she' – rather than the first – 'I'. There may be other restrictions concerning structure, length, and jargon.

Make your style persuasive

A persuasive style encourages people to read material rather than consign it to a shelf. Such a style adopts:

- the active voice
- simple language
- readability
- brevity
- clarity
- lists
- thorough editing.

Active voice

English sentence-construction uses this basic pattern:

$$Subject——Verb——Object$$

To take a simple example: 'I (*subject*) typed (*verb*) the report (*object*).' This is what is called an *active* sentence: the doer

('I') comes first and the thing to which something is done ('the report') comes last. If we make that thing come first, however, the sentence reads very differently: 'The report was typed by me.' This is a *passive* sentence. Passive sentences sound impersonal and less direct than active ones. Here are some more examples:

'This new report is presented by me for your decision.'

'Three attempts were made by me to solve the problem.'

'It will be recognised that...'

The active forms of these sentences put the doer first, and so make them sound more robust:

'I am presenting this new report for your decision.'

'I made three attempts to solve the problem.'

'You will realise that...'

Putting the doer first attracts the reader's attention. Using the active voice is generally more effective, especially in business documents. Good word-processing software can identify where you are using the passive voice and suggest ways to change it.

To alter a sentence from the passive to the active, ask yourself the question 'By whom is *x* being done?' Put this person or thing at the start and follow it with the verb and the rest of the sentence. If you cannot answer the question 'By whom?' then the chances are that the reader will not know who is doing the action and may need to work it out.

Simple language

In business reports complex language is a killer. Experts in a subject tend to adopt it, often unconsciously – for instance when they use jargon. Readers are seldom impressed by complex language. More business communication fails through this than because of insufficient facts. Simplify such phrases as:

- '...in the circumstances...'
- '...the aforementioned situation...'
- '...having duly considered the options...'
- '...we find it incontrovertible that...'.

Aim instead for short sentences without multiple clauses (see *Six infallible ways* on page 36). Also, put statements in a positive and direct form. Tame, colourless, and hesitant writing seldom persuades. If your writing seems uncommitted then that is likely to be how the reader reacts too.

Words like 'but' and 'not' have a cumulative effect, making ideas complex and the message negative. Readers usually prefer being told what is, rather than what is not, the case. In the following list of words, for instance, it is better to use the ones on the right than those on the left:

Weak	Strong
not succeed	failed
not right	wrong
not honest	dishonest

Readability

Broadly, this means that people find it easy to understand and absorb your material. Readability comparisons are usually made against baselines such as a tabloid newspaper, a Dickens novel, a Churchill speech, a life assurance policy, and so on. It is calculated by measuring:

● average sentence length

■ number of 'big' words – those of three or more syllables

▲ complexity of sentence-construction – the number of clauses and subclauses.

How readable is *your* writing? Do you know whether you tend to write long or short sentences, use complex or simple words? Although readability is ultimately a subjective matter, it is always worth testing an important document by using the readability facilities of one of the main word-processing packages. WordPerfect for Windows, for example, can compare your document with any other you select. So if your organisation has produced a particularly well-written report you can assess all your future writing against this standard.

Six infallible ways to write a short sentence

1 **Split and disconnect**
   break it up into two or more sentences

2 **Split and connect**
   put a full stop and start a new sentence with a connecting
   word like 'however' or 'but'

3 **Say less**
   check for repetition and redundancy

4 **Use a list**
   vertical lists break up sentences into manageable chunks

5 **Cut verbiage**
   eliminate excess words and convoluted phrases

6 **Bin it and start again**
   if you can't untangle it, discard and rewrite it

Brevity

Persuasive business documents are usually short, as are
individual sentences and paragraphs. Removing unnecessary
words takes discipline: carefully check to find where you can
substitute one word for two, eliminating any unnecessary
repetition.

Promote brevity by scoring out every alternate word. This
seldom produces a viable document, yet it may highlight words

that can be safely removed without affecting meaning or impact.

Clarity
Mystifying words and phrases include:

● jargon

■ gobbledegook

▲ newspeak

◉ ambiguity.

These have no place in a business document, let alone one meant to be persuasive.

Jargon consists of words belonging to a specialist area with a particular meaning to those in the know. Never assume that because your readers know the jargon they still want to see it. They too will appreciate clarity.

Gobbledegook consists of meaningless sentences and phrases that may look impressive yet, on reflection, do not make sense. Technical reports to management are far too often filled with scientific gobbledegook.

English is one of the most flexible languages in the world. New words are constantly emerging, but *newspeak* consists of contrived expressions possessing a false convenience. 'Decisioning', 'implementability', or 'environmentalism' are all examples of unhelpful newspeak.

In your search for clarity hunt down vaguely expressed ideas and lengthy speculations that leave the reader guessing. These abstractions seldom benefit the persuasive cause.

Similarly, check for *ambiguity*, where what you are saying can be understood or interpreted in several ways. You undermine your persuasiveness by leaving the reader uncertain and having to work out what you mean.

Business readers respond well to words or language with which they are reasonably familiar or comfortable. For example, readers increasingly expect documents to avoid sexism, racism, and other signs of prejudice. To enhance your persuasiveness, be sure that you are speaking the same type of language as the reader.

Lists

Create lists of closely linked items or points. Rather than bundling everything into a single sentence, consider presenting a numbered list or bullet points. For example, earlier in this chapter the following was converted into a bullet list:

'... it also concerns hidden factors such as style, tone, spoilers, appearance.'

' ... it also concerns hidden factors such as:

● style

■ tone

▲ spoilers

◉ appearance.'

Editing

Strong editing can eliminate the above stylistic problems. Allowing yourself sufficient time to do the editing job thoroughly is important, and is discussed further in the following two chapters.

Tone

'I didn't like the way she spoke to me.' Sometimes what people say is less important than how they say it. In written material, an acceptable tone avoids words or phrases that are:

◉ jarring

▣ unacceptable

▲ inappropriate.

For example, a report may be phrased too optimistically, or a sales proposal may be excessively self-promoting or critical of competitors. Similarly, a report might harangue the reader about past decisions or delays in taking action. These may fail to persuade because readers do not like the tone. The facts may be true, yet the tone upsets readers or makes them feel uncomfortable. A useful test for suitability of tone is to ask yourself 'Would I wish to be spoken to like this?'

One of the many benefits of researching your readers is discovering the right tone to adopt. For instance, if you suspect that your reader has little sense of humour, then levity in your document may backfire. Make your tone:

- positive rather than negative
- assertive rather than aggressive
- challenging rather than threatening
- direct rather than indirect
- respectful rather than disrespectful
- polite rather than impolite.

Spoilers

Spoilers are lapses of detail that undermine credibility, sow seeds of doubt, or antagonise. Potentially well-written documents often stumble over:

- poor spelling
- weak grammar
- literals (that is, typing errors)
- discriminatory language
- number usage.

Poor spelling

Although few business readers want outstanding prose, they generally expect you to spell correctly. Spelling mistakes encourage your audience to wonder:

● what other details have been neglected

■ whether the writer has even bothered to check the document.

With modern word processors there is no credible excuse for such errors: use your spell-checker!

Weak grammar

Lapses such as using the singular instead of the plural or the wrong tense can undermine an otherwise persuasive report by irritating the reader and again raising doubts about reliability.

Your document may be read by a stickler for grammar. Managers whose first language is not English and have worked hard to become fluent in it may be particularly irritated to receive reports that reveal weak grammar.

You can obtain considerable help in this area from the best word processors, which will identify many grammatical problems. It is always worth asking someone you trust to read your document to spot this type of spoiler.

Literals

With care, these are easily eliminated; failing to do so undermines credibility. Some typical literals include:

- transposed or additional letters

- transposed words

- misused, misplaced, or missing apostrophes:

    - *it's* (it is) instead of *its* (of it)

    - *their's* instead of *theirs*

    - *theyll* instead of *they'll* (they will)

    - *theyre* instead of *they're* (they are).

Spotting these can be tiresome and explains why care in the final editing stage is essential. A spell-checker may not help if the words themselves are correctly spelt: it will not pick up 'he' as a literal where you meant to type 'the'. However, the best spell-checkers may query your use of a word – by asking, for example, 'Do you mean personal or personnel?' It is wise to ask several people to read your document just for literals.

Discriminatory language

Culture and the nature of the organisation usually determine what counts as discriminatory language. In particular, sexist language is widely unacceptable – and avoidable:

Avoid	Prefer
manpower	workforce, staff, labour power
man-made	synthetic, artificial
chairman	chairperson, chair
man-hours	work hours
master copy	top copy, original
girls, ladies	women

Again, several of the better computer spell-checkers will identify these and offer alternatives.

Number usage
Numbers often play an important role in persuasive documents. Common spoilers are:

● numbers out of context

■ excess numbers

▲ wrong numbers

● lack of pattern.

A number out of context is one of the cardinal sins of persuasiveness, because it leaves the reader wondering how to interpret the information. For example, whether the following is good or bad news depends on your expectations:

Out of context
> Sales rose 12 per cent this month.
>
> We cut overheads this year by 5 per cent.
>
> Production is running at 75 per cent capacity.

Those expectations are clear if more information is provided:

In context
> Sales rose 12% against 24% last month.
>
> We cut overheads 5% this year, compared with only 1% last year.
>
> Production is running at 75% capacity, whereas our target is 95%.

Keep numbers simple to help the reader to make sense of them:

Hard to understand
> Now 56.75% of production is made at night.
>
> Some 34% of those who used the service complained.

Easy to understand
> We make more than half (56.75%) of our production at night.
>
> Over one in three people (34%) using the service complained.

A mass of numbers can be overwhelming, forcing readers to hunt for elusive patterns or exceptions. If you must present many numbers, be sure they tell a story:

● Rank from smallest to largest, or vice versa.

■ Quote averages, not all available data.

▲ Highlight portions of a table using shading, different typefaces, and borders.

● Convert figures into pictures and charts.

Wrong numbers certainly undermine your credibility; the more figures you include, the greater the chance of error. Watch out particularly for:

● wrong totals

■ inconsistent numbers across tables or pages

▲ incorrect percentages

● mistakes in formulas.

Your numbers should tell a story, make an obvious point, or strengthen an argument. Like words, numbers are seldom entirely neutral: their significance depends on who selects them and why. When there is no obvious pattern, readers are left to hunt for it themselves, which reduces persuasiveness.

Ensure that numbered sections or paragraphs are in numerical sequence and that page numbers are also present and correct.

Appearance

Looks alone may not kill your document, yet they can certainly undermine it. Regrettably, readers frequently make judgements using superficial evidence, including how a document is presented. Aspects of appearance to focus on are:

- layout and spacing
- charts and illustrations
- paper and binding
- cover.

Layout and spacing

These help your readers by presenting them with material that is attractively presented and laid out on the page. Use plenty of white space and wide margins. Make the spacing between lines sufficiently deep to give the text a pleasant appearance – usually 1.5-line or 2-line spacing will do. If these create an overlong document, consider reducing the content rather than squeezing the material into a smaller space.

For memos and short reports aim to get everything onto a single page. This 'one-page discipline' forces you to refine your material, even if occasionally you cannot reach this ideal.

Charts and illustrations

Simple, well-presented pictures telling a story can be extremely persuasive. Be creative with your message and make some of it visual, because readers invariably remember such material better than the words. Consider substituting a chart whenever you have a dozen or more numbers to present: this will help to focus your message. However, endless pie diagrams or a succession of dreary bar charts will not enhance your message.

Low-cost computer software now enables everyone to produce professional-looking images. If you cannot make the graphic look professional, leave it out.

Paper and binding

When your printed document is handled by a reader, what kind of impression will it convey? Will it communicate quality, solidity, professionalism? Documents that feel good to hold play a subtle role in building reader confidence. Might a high-grade paper, for example, enhance your document's appearance and feel? Likewise, give some attention to the binding:

● Spiral binding is cheap and easy to handle but does not look impressive.

■ Thermal binding can be costly and may prevent the document from being easily folded open flat, but looks professional.

▲ Off-the-shelf binders can look pleasant but seldom communicate quality.

Choose a binding to enhance your document's appearance.

Cover

Any document of more than half-a-dozen pages deserves its own separate cover page with the title on it. This may sometimes seem excessive, yet it is a useful way of drawing attention to your work.

Consider enhancing the front cover by using a simple illustration and presenting the main title in a bold, attractive way. Most readers will also find it helpful if you indicate on this cover page:

● the current date

■ the subject matter

▲ the main purpose

● the source.

In memos and short items where you do not have a separate title page or cover, state the topic immediately after the date, the name of the author, and that of the recipient.

Titles focus attention on what the material is about and indirectly contribute to persuasiveness. They need to be:

● short

■ easy to understand

▲ a summary of your purpose.

5 detail

Attention to detail underpins persuasive reports or proposals but is often taken for granted. Small yet significant errors that harm persuasiveness often occur in:

- facts
- structure
- logic
- simplicity.

Facts

An army can often retain soldiers in reserve yet still win battles. What counts is how and when those reservists are sent to the front, and their effectiveness once they are there. In the struggle for persuasion, facts are your footsoldiers, yet not all need to be thrown into battle.

Using the right number of facts strengthens the persuasive power of your writing. When you have the right ones, they recede into the background, becoming mere detail within the larger picture of how they are deployed. So what exactly is a fact and how is it best used?

A fact is something known to have occurred, to exist, or to be true. Like soldiers, though, not all facts have the same fighting fitness. Some are stronger, more valuable, or available than others, requiring decisions about:

● quantity

■ quality

▲ combinations

● usage.

Quantity

Inexperienced business writers often assume that the way to persuade is by overwhelming the readers with evidence. Yet sheer quantity is seldom effective: it confuses readers and distracts from the main flow of the argument. Understanding your readers (see also Chapter 3) allows you to:

● use no more facts than are necessary to make your case

■ keep some facts in reserve

▲ consign lesser facts to appendices.

Quality

The quality of a fact or piece of information is ultimately a matter of judgement. Broadly, though, quality means that what you present is reliable, true, or testable in some way, and also that it is *relevant*. Irrelevant facts may be true and look impressive, yet they will not enhance your case. To avoid such irrelevancies, ensure that the facts used:

● advance your argument

■ shed new light on matters

▲ tie in with other facts.

One powerful and relevant fact can be many times as effective as half a dozen interesting but irrelevant ones. In aiming for quality, try reviewing facts against these criteria:

● must know

■ would like to know.

'Must know' facts help convince any reader about the strength of your argument. You cannot omit them without serious damage. 'Would like to know' facts may be informative, even entertaining, yet readers have got to hack through them to reach the underlying argument. Resist the temptation to include 'would like to know' facts; but if you still feel that they should be available, at least consign them to an appendix.

How facts are combined

Even high-quality facts do not simply 'speak for themselves'. How you combine and interpret them matters almost as much as the facts themselves:

- Build a logical sequence of facts.

- Show how they naturally link together.

- Present the most important facts first, not last.

- Avoid linking high-quality facts to low-quality ones.

Where to use facts

It is always a challenge deciding where in a document particular facts fit best. Using all your ammunition in the opening section is weak, and consigning high-quality information to an appendix is wasteful. Try asking yourself regarding each fact that you intend to use:

- Is it a 'must know' or a 'would like to know'?

- Does it advance my case at this particular point?

- Where is its ideal place?

- Would it be better off in an appendix?

Structure

Early in your document, explain:

- what it is about

- how it is organised.

When people read they are continually seeking patterns, clues, and other help to make sense of what they have in front of them. So the structure of a document plays an important role in persuasion. The ideal structure is:

● simple

■ comprehensible

▲ logical.

In complex documents, offer:

● a brief explanation of the structure

■ short introductions

▲ headings

● numbered sections and pages

● previews or overviews

● a contents page

■ conclusions and summaries.

These help readers to begin sorting and classifying information, making it easier to understand a document. The two stages in ordering material suitably are to:

● make sense of it for yourself

■ structure it for the reader.

Make sense of it for yourself

Before you can structure material for the reader, you must first create logical groupings that you yourself find useful. Everyone develops their own way of doing this. Techniques for structuring include:

● generating lists

■ storing and sorting information on cards

▲ mind maps

● telling a story

● drawing symbols or diagrams

● using colours

■ adopting a template structure.

Lists

Benjamin Franklin invented the single-sheet method back in the eighteenth century, and it remains useful today. On one half of the page he would list the 'pros' of an argument and on the other side the 'cons'. Try putting on a single sheet everything that you think should be in your document listed under just two categories – for example, 'must know' and 'would like to know' (see above).

Other list ideas worth using are:

● key information arranged in short bullet points

- material as a numbered sequence

▲ everything categorised under no more than half a dozen headings.

The final structure will emerge naturally once you put material into simple-to-handle lists.

Information on cards

With a wide-ranging assortment of information it can be useful to record each piece of data on its own index card. When you have sufficient cards, you physically sort them into piles until they are in convenient groupings. These form the basis for structuring your document. There is also computer software available to assist in sorting and re-arranging ideas.

Mind maps

These are powerful and easy to use. You start with a single key word or idea which you place in a circle or other shape. You add other key words linked by a line to the central one to create a network of connected ideas. Sometimes called 'spider diagrams', mind maps break the tyranny of presenting information in a linear sequence. By revealing the connection between ideas, they more accurately reflect how the brain works, making many such connections at once. Investigate mind maps if you have not previously encountered them.

Telling a story

Try telling the story of what you want to say in your document, for example as if you were talking to someone on the telephone. This approach may free you to create an attention-holding structure that hangs together logically.

As you allow the story to unfold, you discover natural groupings of information and begin to see how to organise your material. Experiment by talking into a tape recorder and listening to the results – a structure for the actual report may spring out at you.

Drawing symbols or diagrams

Some people do their best thinking when working with pictures, symbols, or charts. Try converting everything you want to say into simple images or icons. If there are too many, it probably means that you can merge some into larger, more sensible groupings.

There is also the storyboard method, which consists of a series of blank squares on which you draw a succession of images conveying your message. The panels show the story in sequence or summarise whole sections of a document. Use mainly images and pictures within the squares, rather than resorting to words. If necessary, however, add a few explanatory words alongside each square.

INSTITUTE OF PERSONNEL
AND DEVELOPMENT

Customer Satisfaction Survey

*We would be grateful if you could spend a few minutes answering these questions and return the postcard to IPD. <u>Please use a black pen to answer.</u> **If you would like to receive a free IPD pen, please include your name and address.***

....

1. Title of book ....

2. Date of purchase: month ....   year ....

3. How did you buy this book?
   ☐ Bookshop   ☐ Mail order   ☐ Exhibition

4. If ordered by mail, how long did it take to arrive:
   ☐ 1 week   ☐ 2 weeks   ☐ more than 2 weeks

5. Name of shop .... Town... Country ....

6. Please grade the following according to their influence on your purchasing decision with 1 as least influential: (please tick)

	1	2	3	4	5
Title					
Publisher					
Author					
Price					
Subject					

7. On a scale of 1 to 5 (with 1 as poor & 5 as excellent) please give your impressions of the book in terms of: (please tick)

	1	2	3	4	5
Cover design					
Page design					
Paper/print quality					
Good value for money					

8. Did you find the book:
   Covers the subject in sufficient depth   ☐ Yes   ☐ No
   Useful for your work   ☐ Yes   ☐ No

9. Are you using this book to help:
   ☐ In your work   ☐ Personal study   ☐ Both   ☐ Other (please state) ....

Please complete if you are using this as part of a course

10. Name of academic institution...

11. Name of course you are following? ....

12. Did you find this book relevant to the syllabus? ☐ Yes ☐ No ☐ Don't know

Thank you!

To receive regular information about IPD books and resources call 0181 263 3387.
Any data or information provided to the IPD for the purposes of membership and other Institute activities will be processed by means of a computer database or otherwise. You may, from time to time, receive business information relevant to your work from the Institute and its other activities. If you do not wish to receive such information please write to the IPD, giving your full name, address and postcode. The Institute does not make its membership lists available to any outside organisation.

2

Publishing Department

Institute of Personnel and Development

IPD House

Camp Road

Wimbledon

London

SW19 4BR

Colours

Another way to evolve a structure is by using coloured highlighters to emphasise certain types of information in your source material. Use different colours to indicate different kinds of groupings. Bring together all material of the same colour and review the implications for the final structure.

Template structure

Sometimes it helps to adopt a pre-determined structure for grouping information. For example, here are two well-tried ones that can provide a consistent approach to organising written information:

Proposals to other organisations

Introduction

Background

Proposal

Cost

About our organisation

Conclusion and next steps

Detailed appendices

Reports and internal proposals

Management summary (preferably one page)

Introduction

Background briefing

Body of report (analysis)

Conclusions

Recommendations

Appendices

Structuring it for the reader
Some organisations insist on using an in-house structure to encourage consistency, with pre-set groupings such as the ones above into which to fit the material. Check whether your readers expect such a pre-defined structure.

If you are looking for a reliable overall structure, there is always the familiar:

● beginning

■ middle

▲ end.

Most management documents benefit from a clear separation into these three stages. For instance, readers genuinely appreciate help with understanding when you are moving from your opening section to the body of the document and when you are ending it.

Add a contents page for documents over more than a dozen pages long.

Summary

You can never assume that your material will be fully read or fully understood, so a management summary is essential for all but the shortest documents. This can be a useful device for clarifying your thinking if you draft it before tackling the actual report. This may seem impossible – how can you write a summary before you have devised the finished document? In practice, by the time you have gathered and read most of your source material you are ready to create at least a first-draft summary.

The discipline of writing the summary before completing the final report encourages you to think through what you really want to communicate. Of course you can amend this summary later to reflect the nature of the final document.

Another popular structural device is to divide your material into:

● situation

▣ implications

▲ resolution.

Rather like telling a story, this type of grouping feels natural, and most material can be fitted into it. You describe the situation, problem, or opportunity and then explain the issues, implications, and so on. Finally you offer a resolution – a way forward.

Introduction

The introduction is an important scene-setter showing why you are writing in the first place. It provides the context for the whole document: part of being persuasive is telling your readers what to expect. This is the place to explain to your readers what structure to expect, which assures them that there is a logical and comprehensible flow of information.

Background

This demonstrates your grasp of an issue, the history of a situation, or the broader issues surrounding the topic. It allows you to range more widely than in the rest of the document and is a useful location for material:

● too important to consign to an appendix

■ likely to clutter up the rest of the document.

Body of the report

This is where you present your analysis, selection of facts, interpretation of evidence, proposals, and so on. Indicate through headings which section the reader is entering. It can be confusing, for example, to find oneself halfway through the body of the document while still under the impression that it is merely part of the introduction.

Conclusions
Effective management reports contain a separate conclusions section combining all the arguments and information presented so far. You explain what might happen next and provide a case for further action or decisions.

Recommendations
In longer reports or proposals, include a separate section summarising all proposals in numbered list form or as a series of bullet points. Although such material may also be partly contained in your opening management summary, this final section reinforces your message:

● Tell readers what you are going to tell them.

■ Tell them.

▲ Tell them what you have told them.

Appendices
These are holding-places for information that would otherwise obscure your persuasive argument. To make the best use of appendices, review:

● material that would best remain in an appendix

■ each appendix for its power to persuade.

Often appendices merely make a document longer without contributing to persuasion, so apply the 'must know'/'would like to know' principle rigorously to appendices (see page 53).

Once you have created your appendices, you may well find that you need not include them at all, in which case you can simply add a note that 'Additional information is available on this issue if required.' And even if you do not expect all your readers actually to read an appendix that you *have* included, consigning material there can still be a useful way to keep the main part of your document short.

Logic

Because logic underpins most business documents, aim for:

● logical connections between one part of a document and the next

■ clear links between one paragraph and the next

▲ natural flow from each set of facts or arguments to another.

Will your readers understand the relationship between disparate bits of information? Illogical associations cause readers to wonder:

● 'Why are you telling me this?'

■ 'Is this connected with that?'

▲ 'Does this follow from what has just gone before?'

● 'On what is this conclusion or recommendation based?'

● 'What evidence supports this argument?'

Persuasiveness often strongly relies on ensuring tight, logical links between arguments. Business readers particularly need to be able to follow causal links: that is, how one thing is connected with something else, and why.

Simplicity

This is a real hidden persuader, underrated and often forgotten. The most convincing documents convey simplicity, even when the subject matter itself is complex. Promote simplicity through:

● frequent summaries

■ eliminating complex phraseology

▲ short sentences

● visual images

● metaphors and similes

● appendices (see above)

■ numbering.

Frequent summaries

These prevent readers from losing track of an argument and also enable them to realise where a document is going. After a lengthy section consider offering a small heading entitled 'Summary so far', or start its final paragraph by offering 'To summarise…'.

Short, regular summaries offer instant updates on where one has reached. They take care of readers, reassuring them that they are following the arguments or understanding the issues.

Eliminating complex phraseology

This is an easy route to simplification. Review your document line by line to find sentences containing several subclauses or communicating several ideas simultaneously. Eliminate jargon even if your readers are familiar with your technical phrases (see Chapter 4).

Short sentences

These consist of around seven to ten words and are relatively easy to achieve with practice. They contribute towards making your document a pleasure to read. But don't overdo it: too many extremely short sentences in quick succession can make writing seem jerky.

Visual images

Charts, diagrams, photographs, drawings, and other pictorial devices can dramatically simplify communication. Consider replacing some of your straight text with visual images.

Enlarged words or huge type are *not* pictorial and seldom enhance simplicity or emphasis.

Metaphors and similes

These powerful simplifiers can play an important role in 'story-telling'. They communicate vividly by using imaginative terms that are not necessarily to be taken literally. For example, in one company a manager used the metaphor of the 'Humpty Dumpty problem' in warning about a certain course of action. Long after the report was accepted, people still referred to the 'Humpty Dumpty problem'.

Numbering

Use simple numbering systems for pages and sections. If you also number paragraphs, avoid creating many layers, such as those in legal documents, which adopt the confusing multidecimal approach, ie:

1

   1.1 *(first section in chapter one)*

      1.11 *(eleventh section in chapter one)*

         1.11.1 *(first subsection to the eleventh section of chapter one)*

Instead, choose a simple numbering system that clearly differentiates each layer, eg:

1

   a

      i)

Alternatively, use a mixture of bullet points and numbers to highlight layers. If you are tempted to use four or more layers, return to the original material and simplify further.

6 enhancers

Enhancers significantly improve the chances of being persuasive and are important ways of gaining attention. They encourage people to respond positively because you:

- seek commitment
- use emotional appeal
- take them on a journey
- state the next steps
- edit and develop the text.

Seek commitment

Explaining your vision of what you want helps readers to decide whether to start to be persuaded. You 'enrol' readers by making them feel a part of the vision, so it makes sense to leave proposals and recommendations sufficiently flexible for them to feel that they still have a part to play. Documents that are excessively 'finished' may leave people feeling powerless and even prompt resistance, so:

- Share your vision of what should happen.

■ Answer the reader's unspoken question: 'What's in it for me?'

▲ 'Enrol' the reader in your vision.

Other enhancers for enrolling readers include the following:

Spell it out
Explain the significance of the action that you are advocating. Demonstrate that what should happen next is important or urgent, or both. Offer evidence to support this claim, showing the consequences of not taking action.

Seek limited commitment
It is usually easier to gain agreement to expend a limited amount of resources rather than demand an immediate, major, long-term commitment. Consider dividing suggestions into manageable bites, perhaps phased over time, so that readers are not overwhelmed.

Suggest resources
Where will the resources come from to do what you are proposing? Don't ignore this issue hoping that someone else will provide the answer. Instead, suggest:

● which budget to use

■ the effect on the budget – that is, other ramifications

▲ phasing expenditure over several financial years

- creative solutions for resourcing.

Clarify the outcome

Explain how the action you propose will lead to the outcome you describe. What is the mechanism linking the decision to the final outcome? For example, in proposing a new remuneration scheme to raise productivity, can you show why the new arrangements will achieve the increase?

Name the improvements

List the improvements that will arise once people commit to your suggestions. People need to understand the benefits of becoming committed to what you are proposing. Make sure that these benefits stand out in your material. Put these in an overall context so that readers receive 'the big picture'.

Justify costs

You will be more persuasive when you justify the costs of any action that you are proposing. For example, will improvements match or exceed the costs of investment? On what grounds can new expenditure be justified – such as market pressures, or an important opportunity?

Anticipate objections

Suggesting changes invariably challenges the status quo.

- What objections might people raise?
- Devise convincing responses to likely concerns.

Make it comprehensible

Persuasion is obviously easier when people fully understand what has to be done. Resistance often arises through not realising what is expected. Break down major actions into smaller, more readily appreciated chunks, and help people to understand how they might be affected. Answer their unspoken concern: 'How will this affect me?'

Explain the evaluation

How will readers know that what you have proposed has been achieved? It is usually easier to gain commitment if you clarify:

- how success will be defined
- how outcomes will be measured.

Add flexibility

A comprehensive document may be impressive yet also exclude anyone else's contribution. If readers feel powerless they may seek excuses for rejecting your document. Build in enough flexibility for people to make a contribution without undermining what you want to achieve.

Emotional appeal

All commitments involve some degree of emotional involvement. An important enhancer is therefore building emotional appeal into a document, so that you reach hearts and not just minds.

You are using emotional appeal, for instance, when you excite your readers or offer reassurance. Few people respond to logic alone: they need to connect with what they are being asked to do (see *The persuasion pyramid* in Chapter 1). Decide whether you want to:

● inspire

■ encourage

▲ support

● provoke

● shock

● energise

■ stimulate

▲ worry

● challenge

● sympathise.

Which emotion do you intend to arouse?

Build in emotional appeal either directly or indirectly. An indirect appeal occurs when you offer a succession of facts and arguments that cumulatively achieve the desired response – for example, if your presentation shocks your readers into realising that action is needed.

Direct emotional appeal may be contained in a specific part of the document, such as the conclusion, recommendations, or introduction. For example, a sales proposal might conclude: 'We are excited at the prospect of working with your company and are totally committed to delivering an outstanding service to you.' Alternatively, a management report might begin by warning: 'It is a matter of great concern that our market share continues to drop dramatically.'

Two factors having an important emotional influence are:

- non-neutral words or phrases
- sharing your own emotions with the reader.

Your choice of words and phrases is important in building emotion into your documents. For example, 'increasing profits' is more emotive than merely 'profits'. Similarly, some words and phrases can lessen impact. For instance, the following words suggest tentativeness and may reduce credibility:

- perhaps
- I'm not sure that...
- maybe
- possibly
- no doubt

- presumably
- it seems that...
- ▲ probably.

When you share how you feel about something you present, you are inviting readers to experience this emotion too.

Some organisations demand documents that are apparently devoid of any emotional overtones: everything is meant to be strictly factual and 'scientific'. Although this restriction encourages people to base their arguments on definite facts, persuasive reports in these situations still rely on subjective choice of information, how that is presented, and the choice of words to make one's points.

Take readers on a journey

Persuasive documents take you on a journey. For example, in the business world the best research reports start by describing the problem, then explain possible solutions, and conclude by suggesting suitable action. Similarly, an effective investment proposal will outline the opportunity, review the implications, and conclude with suggestions on whether or not to proceed.

You create a sense of 'journey' by ensuring that your document moves naturally from one stage to another, so that the reader follows your thinking. This is why merely presenting the facts is insufficient. They need to be linked, so that they gradually unfold your story and bring it to an understandable conclusion. Always be clear in your mind about where you are taking your readers.

Show the next steps

Persuasive reports or proposals are about action, decisions, intentions. Tell your readers what you want to happen next. For example, a successful sales proposal may suggest that readers now buy a service. Alternatively, a management report may seek a clear decision to proceed with launching a new product, initiate research, or sack an employee.

If the reader acted on your document:

● what would be a successful outcome?

■ what exactly would the reader do next:

- call a meeting

- sign a cheque

- invite further submissions

- make a telephone call

- put someone in charge

- give or refuse permission

- make a visit

    – send a memo

    – take no action?

Having obtained and analysed large amounts of information, it can be tempting to leave the task of deciding what to do next to the readers. In business, people need reports and proposals that *explain* the implications for action.

Make it easy for readers to say yes by stating clearly what will be required to take your ideas to the next stage. Sometimes your next steps will merely be a list of suggestions; even so, readers appreciate such help. Consider concluding your documents with a separate section headed 'Next steps'.

Edit and develop

The secret of persuasive documents lies partly in the editing stage. It usually requires several drafts to make a business document fully persuasive, because you require time to:

● obtain and incorporate feedback

■ adjust phraseology

▲ correct spoilers

● improve clarity.

Even when under pressure, create space for this vital editing and refining stage. Though sometimes tedious, it makes a huge difference to whether a document works well. Give yourself time for the editing stage by using the principle: *Don't get it right – get it written.*

Once you have a first draft, no matter how basic, it is easier to develop it further. Many people agonise over how to start their reports and proposals, suffering the tyranny of the blank page. Producing a rough draft frees you from this to write well later, because it hardly matters what the first version looks like. The final one will certainly look different.

Once you have a rough draft you can start experimenting with ways of building in persuasive ideas and identify areas where more information is needed. The early draft may also suggest a new, improved structure. When you have your initial draft you can apply the second principle: *Once it's written – get it right.*

Editing starts with reviewing broad issues such as whether the general story is coming across, the structure, the flow of the material, and the broad contents of each section.

Hunt for paragraphs that do not hold your attention, that flow awkwardly from the previous ones, or that are too long. Ruthlessly change, drop, or move them. Search out and destroy the spoilers (see Chapter 4). This editing stage can be tiresome and indeed seem endless, so be prepared to take a break once in a while. Let someone else read your draft while you have that break by doing something entirely different. You can return later and approach your text as if reading it for the first time.

A sales proposal may pass through half a dozen or more versions. Other reports may go through similar stages, as various people provide input and offer feedback. It is a sign of strength, not weakness, if your document is completely reconstructed and reorganised after the first couple of drafts. Editing is an evolutionary process that is demanding and rewarding. During it, keep reviewing whether:

- your material is retaining the readers' interest

- a particular sentence or paragraph is really essential to your story (see also Chapter 3)

- it seems convincing.

If you have thoroughly edited and developed your document, taking into account the ideas throughout this book, it should be both persuasive and a real source of P-R-I-D-E:

Purpose – **R**eader – **I**mage – **D**etail – **E**nhancers

how persuasive are you? (answers)

1 *More persuasive*: (b)

Principle: It is often more persuasive to quote someone else than to say it yourself.

Reader thinks:

(a) 'This is ritual encouragement.'

(b) 'People are saying that about me? My hard work is being noticed.'

2 *More persuasive*: (b)

Principle: Statements with a 'but' appear negative, suggesting deeper, unexpressed reservations.

Reader thinks:

(a) 'There are severe doubts: we shouldn't proceed, even if the money's available.'

(b) 'The recommender believes in the project.'

3 *More persuasive*: (a)

Principle: Using the original person's wording is a form of 'mirroring' and builds relationships.

Reader thinks:

> (a) 'I do expect it and it will happen.'
>
> (b) 'Can I be sure? Maybe not. My report or yours?'

4 *More persuasive:* (b)

Principle: Mirroring and direct language build confidence.
Reader thinks:

> (a) 'If it's taken that much thought maybe we shouldn't proceed.'
>
> (b) 'This person is keen to proceed now.'

5 *More persuasive:* (b)

Principle: 'Try' implies uncertainty.
Reader thinks:

> (a) 'Has doubts about whether it will be done on time.'
>
> (b) 'This person is glad they've got the project and will do it on time.'

6 *More persuasive:* (b)

Principle: Create a sense of certainty by using 'when' rather than 'if'.
Reader thinks:

> (a) 'This person has doubts as to whether they will get the order.'

(b) 'This person is sure that they will get the job and can produce the results I want.'

7 *More persuasive*: (a)

Principle: Reframing to avoid directly contradicting someone.
Reader thinks:

(a) 'Good point: maybe the new system is unavoidable.'

(b) 'That's what you think; I think otherwise.'

further reading

The following are readable, sensible, and generally useful:

CUTTS M. *The Plain English Guide*. Oxford, Oxford University Press, 1995. (Down to earth and comprehensive.)

BARTRAM P. *Perfect Business Writing*. London, Arrow Books Ltd, 1993. (Short and packed with useful ideas.)

LEIGH A. AND MAYNARD M. *Perfect Communications*. (Chapter 5.) London, Arrow Books Ltd, 1994. (Full of nuggets.)

SERAYDARIAN P. AND PYWELL S. *Successful Business Writing*. Poole, Cassell plc, 1994. (Well presented, with opportunities to check how you are doing.)

The Economist Style Guide. London, The Economist, 1995. (A mine of helpful principles, presented as an A–Z guide.)